MID-BLOOM

poems by

Katie Budris

Finishing Line Press
Georgetown, Kentucky

MID-BLOOM

Copyright © 2021 by Katie Budris
ISBN 978-1-64662-583-3 First Edition
All rights reserved under International and Pan-American Copyright Conventions. No part of this book may be reproduced in any manner whatsoever without written permission from the publisher, except in the case of brief quotations embodied in critical articles and reviews.

ACKNOWLEDGMENTS

Versions of some of these poems have previously appeared in:

"Dawn Paddle" – *Deep Wild Journal* (2021)
"Full" – *From the Depths*, Haunted Waters Press (2014)
"Keeping Things Alive" – *Philadelphia Stories* (2016)
"Leaving Home" – *After Hours* (2005)
"Rain Turns to Snow" – *River and South Review* (2021)
"Relapse" – *The Kelsey Review* (2009)
"Waiting for the Blue Line, Chicago" – *Crossing Lines*, Main Street Rag (2015)

Publisher: Leah Huete de Maines
Editor: Christen Kincaid
Cover Art: Linnea Broling
Author Photo: Katie Budris
Cover Design: Katie Budris

Order online: www.finishinglinepress.com
also available on amazon.com

Author inquiries and mail orders:
Finishing Line Press
PO Box 1626
Georgetown, Kentucky 40324
USA

Table of Contents

5:00pm, Weeknight 1

Backyard Bird Watching 2

Relapse 3

Keeping Things Alive 4

Rain Turns to Snow 6

Turning John Ashbery's "Photograph" into a Ghost Story 7

The First Morning 8

Leaving Home 10

How to Survive a Blizzard 11

Diagnosis 12

When Skies Are Grey 13

Waiting for the Blue Line, Chicago 14

I Thought I Saw My Mother Today 15

Dawn Paddle 16

Chemotherapy, Day 17 17

Mid-Bloom 18

Full 20

Looking Back to Move Forward 21

If Things Were Otherwise 22

Dedicated to Geraldine Budris
Miss you, Mom

5:00pm, Weeknight

I sit at the kitchen table, thirteen
years old and overwhelmed by pre-
algebra. I figure, in about three-and-a-

half minutes my mom will ask me to boil
the potatoes. I'll watch the water, keep
the lid cracked, hum along to *Greensleeves*

playing in the living room, piano
student's fingernails on ivory, the click
of the metronome, mom's pencil, soft

voice counting one-and-a-two-and-a... Soon,
Dad's briefcase will lead him in the door, I
will set the table, Mom will butter

the rolls and Dad will mash the potatoes
just the way I like them, serve dinner on
Mom's floral china, placemats, oak table, grace.

Backyard Bird Watching

Through the kitchen window, I watch
birds perch on the feeder. A few,
I know by name—
red winged blackbird,
yellow finch,
mourning dove.

From the kitchen table, I imagine
catching one, keeping it as a pet,
or befriending it in such a way
that it would return to see me daily,
like a cartoon princess, a sort of
tamer of wild creatures.

Or maybe, I could fly away myself.
I imagine my house from a bird's-eye view,
a flat, gray rectangle among rectangles
The woods, a smattering
of dark green, local park stretched below
still smaller than I'd ever realized.

I wonder how I'd find my way
home, how these wild birds always
knew how to find our little yellow birdhouse,
stone bath. Do they worry they'll never find
the right rectangle again? Or do they simply trust—
if they never return here—

someone else will feed them.

Relapse

Behind closed doors, she is 19 again.
Cracks a window and breathes suburban air—
fresh, deep, easy. Props an elbow
against crisp eggshell walls, bare toes crinkling
around powder blue bath rug. Lights. Drags. Ashes
in the toilet. Forgets her smooth scalp, swollen
calf. Eyes closed, she remembers her first
apartment, above the Blue Moon
Café, Friday nights with her baby
spinning her polka dot skirt silly across
the dance floor, his fingers catching the love bug
all over again in her short red curls. She flicks.
Unaimed ash finds her knee, early 50s, carrying the weight
of children, cancer, the cha-cha. Putting out
the cigarette she zips up evidence. Tucks away
worn cloth makeup case in the middle drawer. Pops a mint. Heads
down the hallway. Takes the stairs one
by one. Slowly.
Aching

Keeping Things Alive

It is December, and our window ledge
is lined with plants—

bamboo shoots, devil's ivy, an elephant bush,
two cacti, one orange, one yellow, and

a large rhododendron shadowing two new
sprouts. We've collected these

over two-and-a-half years, purchased
new pots and soil, tried different windows

and porches to identify the right combination
of direct and ambient light.

We thought we had the balance
figured out. But as I put away the watering can

just before bed on an unusually
cold night, I notice the fishbowl

beside the plants appears still and vacant.
Our deep blue Betta, hidden from view,

takes minutes to find, motionless, belly
up inside his toy castle. I pause.

My eyes fill gently like
the trays beneath the pots, like

the fishbowl itself. I am alone in this
moment—you have been fast asleep for hours.

I set down the watering can, leave
the dead fish, write a note on the fridge

for you to find in the morning.
All I can manage are

the heaviest words I've ever scribbled—
I'm afraid all the plants are dying.

Rain Turns to Snow

Like the last day
I would see you. Smiling—

Wheels skidding on ice
as I push you from parking lot

to in-patient. Your hand
suddenly becomes a child's

slipping out of its protective
mitten, palm catching

the flakes, twisting
with awe as if the air carries

radiation. Your eyes reflect
in icicles dangling

off doorways. I pause, there,
creeping up the sidewalk

despite bitter cold, try to memorize
your face, reborn, healed

by snow, so that later,
as I watch you die,

watch your breath become
ice, slowing, freezing, I

will remember you
like this. In wonder.

As if you know.
As if comforting me

in advance, saying—"Now, now.
There, there."

Turning John Ashbery's "Photograph" Into a Ghost Story

You might like to live
in one of those smallish cities
with one stoplight where you can walk
to the grocery store, or the barber
but sometimes
you drive anyway, out of habit.

Houses climb the hill, then fumble
with apartments and trailer homes and that
old, abandoned cottage with a swinging
for sale sign, something out of a
Stephen King novel. The wood
paneling peels white paint that looks
more like rainy-day-grey and the porch
buckles and creaks on eighty-year-old knees.

But let's step back to the beginning, as if
nothing happened. Just you in your new
small-town house, picket fence and casserole
dinner with that new neighbor who makes
concessions and avoids looking
west at that hill and that cottage.

In a minute the neighbor will go home
and the clock's ticking will make you rethink
the small town, the grocery story, the driving.
You'll put on your scarf
and take a walk through the crisp, thin air.
The fall trees flame on and the wind
scrapes away at the side of the cottage
as you hurry past. The wind, a steel
scouring pad on the porch posts,
on your pale cheeks' skin.

The First Morning

I wake in my own bed for the first time
after weeks downtown, six people

in one hospital room, taking turns
on the cot and sharing the pull out.

At home again, I am alone, and the whole
house is silent. I fixate on the ceiling

fan blades, spinning backwards
to circulate the air, chain swinging, almost

clacking against the light cover, but not.
Sun streaks through the slats

of the blinds so I know it's almost noon,
but I don't want to get out of bed.

You are not here.

Downstairs, in the kitchen, your
kitchen, there must be people gathering:

my siblings, all married and moved out,
their spouses and kids, maybe neighbors

bringing casseroles and comfort,
and a priest, likely Father Joe even though

he's new, and never knew you.
I've never done this

before. Said goodbye
forever. So while I'd like to choose

songs and readings, photos, ways
to remember, I'd rather stay

in bed, where for years I've woken
to the sound of your soft knock and

"Good morning, good morning—time for school!"
Or your students' piano lessons, melody of *Greensleeves*

mingling with your voice in the room below.
Other mornings, the sound was your laughter

shared with girlfriends over coffee. Even in
so much silence, there isn't much room

for laughter. Just an empty hospital bed
for no-longer-needed long-term care

a list of final advice—faith and a smile
are the most important things—

my father and me, his teenage daughter,
left with the question of how to be

just two.

Leaving Home

I.
She thinks
if she takes her shoes
off at the door, the green
beach grass world will stay
outside and she can live
in black and white.

II.
Shag carpet tickles
her ankles, invites her to lie
down with a pillow and rainbow
knit afghan, but she
never could
sleep to silence.

III.
In the morning, she
wonders why the window
was left crack open, snowy
March leaking in, dripping
between the peel of wallpaper,
and freezing.

IV.
Crossing lines built
by frozen breakfast food and
oak kitchen tables, she leaves
her leftovers behind. Forgets dishes
undone, door open, lawn not
mowed, growing into the sand.

How to Survive a Blizzard

Outside, snow buries this Midwest winter,
the only remaining inhabitants a family
of cardinals, the ones who have been living
in the tree beside the window.

As the wind wages war,
biting through skin and feathers,
the bold red cardinals belly down
beneath the snow. They know

the best protection from a blizzard is not
to fly, but to burrow, escaping
the elements by surrounding themselves
in a cave to keep warm, wait out the storm.

Diagnosis

I did not know you when
you told me to undress,
smashed my left breast.

Turn your head to the side,
you said, so that I was looking away
while you stood behind me, silent.

I did not know why you led me
to a private room where another
would take over, stick me.

I did not know how to respond
when you asked me to describe
what I felt beneath my skin:

Brussel sprout.
First time.
No history.

You spoke no more words, but
when you touched my arm and smiled
softly, eyes glistening wet like mine,

I knew exactly what you were saying.

When Skies Are Grey

Every time I came whimpering in,
red trickling down my leg, kneecap pebbled
and elbows bruising,
you'd mix the perfect ratio
of vanilla and root
and settle me down on the couch.

Somehow you always knew
the perfect cure
for a sidewalk scrape
was a black cow.

I'd sip, lay my head on your lap
and stare out the sliding doors
to the green backyard. That float
and your hand on my back—a band-aid
for a summer day gone wrong,
your soft humming,
the brightest sunshine.

Waiting for the Blue Line, Chicago

> *"Vertigo is something other than the fear of falling. It is the voice which tempts and lures us."*
> Milan Kundera, The Unbearable Lightness of Being

She toes the line—coarse
and yellowed on the concrete—
keeps feet planted, leans
out over the colored stripe,
a construction crane, 145
degree angle.

She wonders whether
she could see the train coming
better from down there—
white cyclops barreling
out of the darkness,
streaking towards her, breaking
borderlines. She wonders
if the electrical current is running
through them, even now—
ominously quiet?

The underground tunnel still
dark, she still leaning, looks down
the worn, rusted tracks
two rails on each side of a damp
channel of water, chewed
gum, lost papers.

I Thought I Saw My Mother Today

Sitting in the snow, head like a peach,
fuzzed, reading the newspaper.

Her story—
surviving are
her husband,
four children,
four grandchildren—

just one column inch
in an otherwise broadsheet newspaper.

I wanted to pull out my pen
and correct the obituary,
change four grandchildren to eight,
wanted to write into the margins,
the names of all the people
who remember her, the ones
she knew and those she didn't
but who know her students, know
her neighbors, know me, know my sister,
know her eldest granddaughter, know
her cancer is not
the end of her story.

Dawn Paddle

When the alarm sounds, it's still too dark
to see if there are slugs in our shoes.
We unzip the tents, pull on damp socks
and empty shoes, break camp by yellow-glow
of flashlight lanterns, and carry our packs
to the shore. One by one, we flip canoes,
slide their aluminum noses into the water,
load up and crawl in.

The lake is still, ever so gently lapping
the canoe, barely pushing back against
my paddle. We move slowly, single-file,
our three canoes followed by another
group of three, group of four. Ten total
slicing through the darkness, sliver
of moon above. Cicadas sing
to us as we paddle. I lean back and look up—
blanketed by deep blue sky with ten thousand
pin pricks of stars, like dots made by
a hummingbird trying to escape
toward daylight.

Somewhere in the silence, a glow
emerges. We pass through tall lake-grass
in the fog, watch for moose, keep lips
pressed shut. Purple precedes pink
and amber until finally, sun-fire breaks
the horizon, outlining pine trees, shimmering
water-surface in all directions. Morning comes.
We are no longer silent out of exhaustion
or necessity. Just awe. Creation. Peace.

Chemotherapy, Day 17

Under brassy bathroom light, patches
of white scalp reflect off my left side part.

I slide my hand across my head, flip
the part to my right. No better. A clump

comes out in my fingers, and I watch
as it joins the pile in the sink—a nest,

tangled among water droplets.
Electric hair clippers in hand, I turn

from the mirror, breathe. My husband
sits on the edge of the bed, hands

clasped, unsure whether to help,
watch, or leave me be. Our eyes

lock, and without warning,
hot salt-tears stream down my face.

We meet between the closets
and he holds me, heaving, eyes

pressed to his shoulder, gasping
for breath. A minute later, I compose

myself, send him away. I retrieve
the clippers from the floor and fix

my gaze to the mirror, flick
the switch, and shave.

Mid-Bloom

My whole adult life, I have failed to keep
a plant alive beyond a few months.
Aloe and cacti have fared best,
desert climate plants requiring little water,
inconsistent attention. And now this
Devil's Ivy, going on a year, purchased
for the promise that it's easy
to care for. It's summer, our first
married and living in the suburbs, grown-up
apartment with a private porch. I have filled it
with foliage—a mixed pot of Coleus, small
sample of English Ivy, my husband's favorite,
and a rail planter with bright red-orange flowers
I can't remember the names of, and
a leafy green plant that seems
to be trying to take control.

With my hands in the dirt, I'm back
on Dawes Street with Mom, planting
Marigolds and Petunias in the yard.
As young as five years old, I'd beg to help,
put on the oversized floral print gardening gloves,
stick my shovel into the earth, and force
out a handful, just enough to place
the perfectly shaped square of soil
from the plastic container into the ground. I'd give up
on the gloves, use my bare hands to wave
away worms, pack the dirt
around our new annuals. Even then, she trusted me
to space the flowers, to choose
which color came next, to pull the blooms
gently from the next box
and tuck it into the flower bed.

I'm not sure where in the last thirty years I lost
my green thumb. But there
in the backyard, my mother knew
I was capable, nurturing, and strong. As if
she knew I would be on my own
much too young when she left this world
much too soon, a flower mid-bloom,
unseen disease spreading from the inside,
slowly growing, then wilting.

Full

> *"and still we are not touching,*
> *like things in a poorly done still life"*
> Billy Collins, "Still Life"

And in the space beneath the plate, I trace
the grain of oak, finger the fraying edge

of holiday placemats, red and green thread
sprawled before me. I light

two centerpiece candles (broken
wick on the third), shake out

the match and lay it beside
my fork and knife, eye the phone,

as if willing it to ring.
Even the flames appear still

against the background of
an empty chair.

Looking Back to Move Forward
after Li-Young Lee's "The Other Hours"

In these quietest moments the water
rests in pause, swirling until the next breeze
or disturbance urges a decision:
push beyond rocks and carry sediment or
boil over, eroding shore.

I think about the little yellow house
lined with orange daylilies, that thin
avenue of trees, the shallow creekbed
separating me
from the slowly dipping sun.

Someone inside me begins clicking
her tongue, like the sound of a bat
cracking the baseball outside
a kitchen window, the cheering crowd,
the soft roar of childhood games
lightly muffled by those trees
and the creek to the west,
the inconsistencies of the day—
one minute, bubbling with delight,
the next, rushing with actuation.

If Things Were Otherwise
> "I got out of bed
> on two strong legs.
> It might have been
> otherwise."
>
> Jane Kenyon, "Otherwise"

I'd follow the scent of Sanka and coffee cake
down the stairs, into the kitchen, like so many
mornings when I'd find you with friends.
But this time, it's just you and me
with cups of coffee, cake, chemo.
You wear your bandanna over peach fuzz,
never bald, and sip from a *Best Mom* mug,
smile. My head is cold and smooth
and I tilt it to one side as questions
spill from my lips—

                does the smell
of butternut squash make you sick? Do your
bones ache from the inside out, pulsing
without warning? Are you sweating
in your sleep and shivering all afternoon?
Does your belly feel like fire smoldering
incessantly? Is the swelling in your
left leg like my left arm, like
a bowling pin, wide and weighted?

You can't answer, of course, you've been gone
twenty years. Still you've never felt closer,
connected by cancer. If you were here,
I'd tell you it's okay to be afraid, to let anxiety
break the smile on your face, to smoke the cigarettes
outside of the bathroom. I'd want you to know
that my fifteen-year-old self might not
have understood, but that I do
now, could have tried, then.

In the silence, I can almost see you
smile, shrug, framed by the bay window
and lush green trees. You'd tilt
your head, say, *it's always something*.
This time, I'd tilt my head, too.
This time, we're both cancer patients.
This time, I'd understand.

Katie Budris holds an MFA in Creative Writing from Roosevelt University and a BA in English from Hope College. Her poems have appeared in literary journals including *After Hours Press, The Albion Review, Border Crossing, Deep Wild Journal, From the Depths* (Haunted Waters Press), *Kelsey Review, Our Time Is Now, Outside In, Philadelphia Stories, River and South Review, Temenos Journal, Yellow Medicine Review*, and the anthology *Crossing Lines* (Main Street Rag). Her debut chapbook, *Prague in Synthetics*, is also available from Finishing Line Press (2015). She was the recipient of a John Woods Scholarship to attend the Prague Summer Program in 2005, and was nominated for an AWP Intro Journals Award in 2004. Currently, Katie is a Senior Lecturer in the Writing Arts Department at Rowan University where she serves as Editor in Chief of *Glassworks* literary magazine and as advisor for *Avant*, the undergraduate student literary magazine. She is a breast cancer survivor and volunteers as a Young Advocate with Living Beyond Breast Cancer. Katie lives in South Jersey with her husband, Chris, and their English Mastiffs, Harper and Winnie. *www.katiebudris.com*

www.ingramcontent.com/pod-product-compliance
Lightning Source LLC
LaVergne TN
LVHW041519070426
835507LV00012B/1689